PUBLIC SPΕAKING PANIC

HOW TO GO FROM STAGE FRIGHT TO STAGE-READY IN LESS THAN 24 HOURS

CODY SMITH

Thank you for choosing this book to guide you in crushing your speech in less than 24 hours.
As an appreciation, I would love to give you a few free gifts.

The Public Speaking Panic Quick Start Checklist.
This is the checklist I walk all my coaching clients through.
With it, you will discover how to implement the contents of this book even faster.

I also want to give you a copy of my bestselling book:
Stage Fight – How to Punch Your Fears of Public Speaking in the Face!

Either go to this URL:https://
fearpunchingcody.com/publicspeakingpanicchecklis
t
or use the QR code for your free gifts:

You can also simply text **PANIC** to (678) 506-7543
to download your free Quick Start Checklist along
with my bestselling book.

CONTENTS

INTRODUCTION

Public speaking is scary, and it's absolutely terrifying when you have little time to prepare. As a public speaking coach, I typically work with people with short deadlines to showtime. Most people don't proactively seek out coaching in the hopes that it comes in handy in the future. Instead, they seek out help in a panic, just shy of it being too late.

As a coach, I can only help so many people one-on-one (there are only so many that can afford the fee to work with me), which is why I created this book. To help as many people as possible. To be your coach for the next twenty-four hours.

It's short and structured in a way to get you from scared and panicked to confident and ready in less than twenty-four hours. That's an incredibly short time frame to get you prepared, but don't think there are any shortcuts to seeing results.

If you put into action the steps laid out in this book, you will be blown away from the transformation—but only if you do the work in the order that's laid out. What's ahead are the right steps in the right environments to maximize the time you spend preparing for your talk.

If you skip steps, you're skipping your chances of actually seeing results.

This is not a motivational book to get you pumped about public speaking. This is a bare essential guide to get you ready, even if you have nothing prepared.

There is literally no time to lose.

Set reasonable expectations

Why you picked up this book, I don't know. The reasons will vary just like the reasons my clients come to me for help when they are in a pinch:

- You've accepted a job or promotion that requires you to speak in front of a crowd often.

- Someone close to you has passed away and you are expected to give the eulogy.
- You have put off working on a presentation, hoping it would get canceled or that someone else would do it.
- You are now obligated to speak for whatever reason on short notice.
- You're the best man or maid of honor for a wedding and you found out the day before the reception that you are expected to give a speech.
- You are filling in for someone who is supposed to speak.
- [Insert your reason here]

Regardless of the reason, the desired result is the same: escape the stress of having to speak with little time to prepare and perform like someone who has their act together.

You will not be amazing in less than twenty-four hours to prepare. It's just not going to happen. I can transform clients who spend a day with me one-on-one. I can even make "miracles" happen with a weeks' notice. But one day just isn't enough time to make a fearful, unprepared speaker ready to perform at a high level, especially not through a book. If you are expecting this book to guide you from nothing to standing ovation, you will be highly disappointed.

That type of thinking is completely unrealistic. It poops on the years of effort professional speakers have put into their craft. Most importantly, it sets unreasonable expectations on you.

So first, set reasonable expectations. You won't be incredible but you can go from a fast-approaching nervous train wreck to comfortably uncomfortable. You may very well still feel nervous leading up to your speaking. That's 100 percent okay. Professionals still get that same feeling before speaking. This book will not take that feeling away. Instead, it will show you how to perform while still nervous, under pressure, and scared when the floor is yours.

That's what you ultimately want, and that's what I want for you: to speak under stress.

Anyone can perform when they are calm and comfortable, but not everyone can handle the rigors of speaking proficiently when all of the attention falls on them. That is exactly what this book will do for you. It will take some effort on your part but you knew that already. Get ready to jump in and start implementing the steps as you discover them, not when you finish the book.

Brace yourself for what's ahead. Less thinking more doing.

The clock starts now.

How to use this book

This is not your typical book that you need to read from cover to cover. There are a number of different paths to choose from depending on your individual needs. Someone using this book to prepare to give a best man's speech at a wedding is going to take a completely different path versus someone who is preparing a quarterly business meeting with presentation slides versus someone reading off a script at an awards banquet.

The first half of the book is about putting together your speech. The second half helps you prepare to deliver the speech. If you've already put together your speech and just need practice presenting it, great! You get to skip the first half.

Everything is written under the assumption that you have very little time to prepare. Even though you are expected to make time in your schedule to prepare, the steps in this book do not assume you have an entire twenty-four hours to devote to putting together a talk and prepare to deliver said talk. The steps assume you also need to sleep, eat, run errands, work your day job, commute, spend time with family, and whatever else you need to get done between now and when you speak.

So to accomplish everything in a short time, you will be pushed to the next step before you will feel ready for the next step. That's by design. If at any point you want to stay on a certain step to make it perfect, stop what you are doing and move on to the next step. The steps are designed so that when you step on stage to give your talk, you'll laugh because it will feel like a piece of cake compared to what you've been through in the previous twenty-four hours.

WARNING: Your scenario may not fit perfectly within the guidance in this book. That's to be expected. You will need to use your best judgement within the gray area. If every scenario possible were captured, this book would no longer be able to address its #1 priority: help people prepare to speak within twenty-four hours. It's been kept short to ensure you get just what you need to start implementing as you discover each step that applies to you.

There is literally no time to lose.

If you are starting from scratch, meaning you have nothing prepared, no slides to give a presentation, nada, zilch, nothing, then go to chapter 1. Stop reading and go!

If you have a script already, go to chapter 5.

If you know what you're going to talk about, meaning you at least have an outline of your speech, but require slides for a presentation, go to chapter 6.

If you have slides to present but have no idea how you are going to present them, go to chapter 7.

If you have an outline of what you are going to say and you don't need slides, go to chapter 8. Move!

It's time to get to work. Let's go!

STARTING FROM SCRATCH

I f you are here, I'm assuming you've got next to nothing to work with. That's perfectly fine, but you can't waste any time moving forward.

Do you at least know what you're talking about? As a maid of honor, you are obviously going to talk about the bride and groom.

For a eulogy: the deceased.

Accepting an award: yourself.

Class presentation: either an assigned topic or a topic of choice.

Defending your thesis: your research.

Asked last minute to speak at a conference: a topic related to the theme of the conference.

It is rare that you don't know what you're talking about at all. If it's completely up to you, then pick something you're either very interested in or very familiar with and move on. You don't have a lot of time to waste here.

If your speech/presentation requires you do some research on the topic, you will either do that now or after the next step depending on how well you know the topic. If you already know quite a bit about the topic, but may need to dig a little deeper to research a few gaps, then go straight to chapter 3.

If you hardly know the first thing about your topic, you need to do the research first. Go to chapter 2.

If you're working with already made slides and will create the outline from that rather than from research or your own knowledge, then go to chapter 7.

HOW TO RESEARCH LIKE A MAD SCIENTIST

L ab coat, wild hair, thick rubber gloves, questionable hygiene, eccentric, lack of ethical morals, excessive uses of electricity with all lab experiments. You know: mad scientist. They waste no time getting lost in endless holes of research. They find exactly what they need and implement immediately without a second thought. They take action far more than they stop to think through what they are doing, throwing caution to the wind. Their methods may be haphazard (or straight-up dangerous), but we can learn a thing or two from their approach to getting things done.

You will want to research with this main goal in mind: quickly find what you need to get started and forget the rest.

Set a clock/stopwatch for thirty minutes (no more than an hour) and start your research.

If you are able to research on your own using readily available resources, abide by the time restrictions. If your research and fact-finding involve other peoples' expertise like a colleague/co-worker, hunt them down immediately and start asking them questions. This may require you to go past your time limit.

When you are researching online, keep in mind that you are looking for main topics to fill in the body of your speech. That means skimming articles, blogs, or research papers for content to quickly determine your main points. This is done quickly by simply reading section headings within those articles, blogs, or research papers to determine what could be useful and what can be ignored. If a section heading looks like it could make up one of your main points, jot it down on a piece of paper and move on to finding the rest of your main points. If you have the option to determine how many main points you need, keep it at three main points. Three points will be significantly easier to remember for you and your audience.

Once you have determined the main points that will

work well together for your speech, start digging into and digesting the information you found related to those main points. Ignore everything else.

Write down those main points and a few sub-points underneath them on a piece of paper as you consume the info you find. You will use this in the next exercise.

To-do Checklist:

- Set a time limit for your research
- Hunt down people to ask questions (if applicable)
- Research your topic
- Write down the main/sub-points

Go to the next chapter.

HOW TO GET EVERYTHING OUT OF YOUR BRAIN AND ONTO PAPER FOR YOUR TALK

I t's time to brain barf everything you know about your topic and get it out on paper. All your knowledge, experience, and related stories, and any findings from your research you completed in chapter 2 (if applicable) will be used as potential material. All the Dorito crumbs of knowledge in between the couch cushions of your brain will now see the light of day.

What you'll need:

1. A piece of paper—the bigger the better
2. The main/sub-points from your research (if applicable)
3. A marker—a pen or pencil is fine but a

marker will serve you better for this exercise. You'll see why in a second.

Go get them now and come back.

With your paper and marker in front of you, write the topic you're talking about dead center on the page and draw a circle around it.

If you did research prior to this step, the first thing you'll do is add your research topics before moving on to adding everything else. Write the first main point you found in your research next to the topic, draw a circle around it, and draw an arrow from the topic of the speech to this new bubble. Do that for each main point (MP) from your research along with any sub-points (SP) you found as well. It could look something like this:

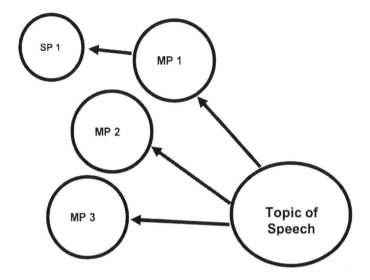

Next, brain barf all over it with everything else that comes to mind about that topic.

Write the first thing that comes to mind next to the topic, draw a circle around it, and draw an arrow from the topic of the speech to this new bubble. This first thought could be a fact about the main topic, a question you have about the main topic, an experience you have related to the main topic, etc. Whatever comes to mind, write it down, do not judge. Just transfer it to paper.

As soon as you are finished connecting the main topic to your first thought, write the next thought that comes to mind, circle it, and connect it with an arrow. Every thought should map back to the main topic.

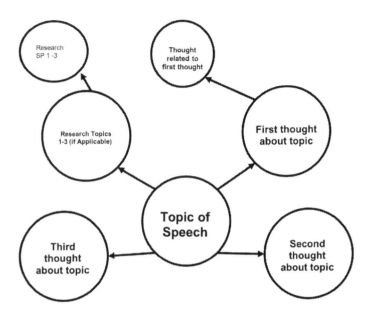

Pro Tip:

As you go through your mind map exercise, do any stories come to mind? Any past experiences that relate to your topic that you can use in your talk? Having stories thrown into your speech is one of the best ways to share a message or make a point and serves several purposes:

1. Makes the speaker more relatable/personable

2. Makes great introductions and closing remarks

3. **Most importantly, you do not have to use up precious time memorizing them**

You simply have to recall those experiences. Stories are a professional speaker's secret ninja weapon. Once you realize just how easy they are to use in your talk, how easily they can allow you to connect with your audience, and how easy they are to speak on, you will become a storytelling machine. I don't give talks without using stories anymore. Without them, speaking is like intentionally playing a game on hard mode. If a story comes to mind while working on your mind map, write it down.

Keep writing down everything that comes to mind until you've exhausted all of your knowledge on the subject. Using a marker forces you to write in broad terms instead of writing every little fine detail. Save the fine details for when you speak.

Here's a quick example. Let's say apes were holding a conference and last minute, King Kong canceled on the meeting planners as the keynote. Panicked, they reach out to me to be a last-minute replacement to give a keynote on my basic level of knowledge on bananas. What's the first thing I do?

Panic.

What's the second thing I do?

Mind map about bananas.

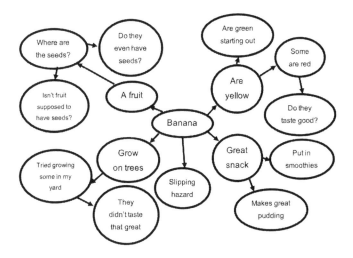

The first thought was that they are yellow so I wrote it down, circled it, and drew an arrow to it. That thought made me think of how they start out green so I wrote that down, circled it, and drew an arrow to it from its parent thought which was that they are yellow. I kept at it until I had exhausted my knowledge about bananas (which I cut short for the sake of this example).

You can see that I had facts, experiences, stories, and questions in my mind map. Now go and do the same for your topic.

If you are doing a mind map for a best man speech, you could write down embarrassing (but tasteful) stories about the groom, how long you've known the groom, how they acted when they first started dating the bride, and why they are the perfect match for each other.

A eulogy would bring to mind memories of the deceased, what made them special, what they meant to you, what they taught you, and how you'll remember them.

If you are doing an ice breaker as a new employee of a company, you'd talk about your work experience, your hobbies, your interests, and possibly what you are looking forward to as a new employee.

You get the picture, start mind mapping. Once you are done, go to chapter 4 to organize the mess.

* * *

To-do Checklist:

- Get a piece of paper and something to write with

Create your mind map using:

- stories
- facts
- experiences
- your research
- Etc.

HOW TO STRUCTURE A SPEECH LIKE A PROFESSIONAL

So you completed your mind map, which I can only imagine looks like a complete mess. You're now going to transform that into an outline that you can actually use for your talk. You will need another sheet of paper for your outline. At the top, leave some room (a few inches) for the outline of your introduction which we'll finish later. Underneath, write the first main branch and any sub-branches before moving to the next main branch. Here's what the banana outline looks like. Notice how it doesn't have a lot of words? The words used on your outline should be the minimum amount needed to jog your memory about what you have planned to talk about.

The reason to have just enough to get by is your

outline is one of the few items you should ever memorize for a speech. The more you cram into your outline, the harder it will be to commit it to memory.

Bananas (main topic):

- Are yellow (main branch)
- Are green starting out (sub-branch)
- Some varieties are red
- Do they taste good? (sub-sub-branch)
- A fruit
- Where are the seeds?
- Do they even have seeds?
- Isn't fruit supposed to have seeds?
- Grow on trees
- Tried growing some in my yard
- They didn't taste that great
- Great snack
- Put in smoothies
- Makes great pudding
- Slipping hazard

You are going to do the same thing with your mind map. Get to work and make your outline and come back when you are done.

Post research

So you've made your mind map and your outline but your mind map exercise led to a few questions you need answered to complete your talk. Find those answers now but only if they will benefit your talk. Write your answers on your outline and move on.

For my banana outline, I had a question about red bananas. I know nothing about them, so if talking about red bananas was pertinent to my talk, I'd do a quick deep dive into these darn red bananas and add what I found out into my outline. If it's not important to my talk, that would get purged and I'd move on.

If the answers you're finding are not clear or you are struggling to find answers, make a judgement call as to whether spending more time searching is worth it.

Purge and organize

With your outline complete, you now need to purge and organize the info. You should have more than what you need to give your talk. Identify the content in your outline you want to keep (like three main points you can talk about) and strike through the rest.

With your main content remaining, decide what order you will bring up each point. This can be in chronological order, sequential, or whatever order makes the most sense to you and your talk.

Once you've purged and organized, go to the top where you left the space and write in the structure of your introduction. This can come in many different flavors, depending on why you're speaking. In some cases, a quick introduction of who you are followed by jumping right into the body of your speech is appropriate. In other cases, an introduction of who you are, why you're speaking, what you are going to speak about, and why the audience should care will be required. I'm counting on you to use your best judgement on how best to start your speech. Write at the top what you believe is needed/required.

At the bottom, you'll write the structure of your conclusion. Again, this will be different based on the reason why you're speaking. Your conclusion could be a summary of your main points, closing thoughts, a call to action, asking for another round of applause for the bride and groom, or a thank you for the opportunity to speak. Lots of options here. If you need to rewrite your outline on another piece of paper after purging and organizing it, do it now.

Moving forward, consider your outline to be a living document, meaning it's going to change. At this point, you have not even used it to guide you through your talk. Your outline is simply a plan for your speech. Plans are great until you put them into action and realize you need to make changes. That's perfectly normal and to be expected.

If you're creating a script from your outline, go to the next chapter. Only do this if you are required to have a script. If you are not required to have a script and just want one to ease your nerves of having to speak and you don't need slides, proceed with just your outline to chapter 8.

If you do need slides made, go to chapter 6.

To-do Checklist

- Make your outline
- Leave room at the top for the introduction
- Finish any needed research and add that info to your outline
- Purge content that's not needed
- Organize your outline so it flows from start to finish
- Add in your introduction
- Add in your conclusion

5

WORKING WITH SCRIPTS

S cripts. **I'm not a fan of scripts.** Scripts are not public speaking. Scripts are public reading. They either force you to never take your eyes from the page, giving the audience a view of only the top of your head, or they force you to do this bobble-head maneuver, constantly looking up at the audience and then back down at the page.

Sometimes, they are a necessary evil. If you are using a script and you were not the one who wrote it, I would encourage you to ask if you can change it to fit your style. Odds are, it uses different sentence structures and pacing compared to how you would naturally speak. Reading it out loud will quickly point out anything that just doesn't sound right.

Change it if you can to something that will sound more natural coming from you.

Your goal will be getting so familiar with the script that you hardly need it. You want to be able to look at your audience way more often than you ever look down at the page.

If you are turning your outline you made in chapter 4 into a script, now is the time to do that. Use your outline to guide you as you write or type out your script from start to finish. Do not waste time trying to make it perfect. It will change significantly as you practice speaking through it. So no need to perfect what will soon change. Write out your script and come back.

Once you are done, split up your script into manageable chunks and highlight the first sentence of each chunk (just as I've done in this chapter). These highlighted sentences will be the structure of your script's outline. They will also help you navigate your script when you look back down at your page to find your place.

Whenever you see the word "outline" in the chapters ahead, assume it's referring to the sentences

you highlighted in your script or if you didn't write a script, then it is your actual outline.

Now take your script and if you need to make slides, then go to chapter 6; if not, go to chapter 8.

To-do Checklist:

- Turn your outline into a script (if applicable)
- Separate your script into manageable chunks
- Highlight the first sentence of each chunk

6

THOU SHALL NOT MURDER THY AUDIENCE

E ver heard of the phrase death by PowerPoint? It's a slow, agonizing death from lethal concentrations of boredom. What's the source of this monstrosity? Presentation slides that look like someone copied and pasted the Bible on them while the speaker read them word for word as if the audience was illiterate.

It should be a crime.

This chapter is going to help you save time making slides and save you from becoming the Grim Reaper of lectures.

Here are a few rules to follow:

1. Your slides are not for you; they are for your audience.
2. Your slides shall not be used as a script for you to read from.
3. Your slides shall not look like you copied and pasted chapters of a book on each slide. If at any point you find yourself making the font smaller to fit all of your precious words on the slide, you are doing it wrong.
4. You shall not tie your worth into the number of slides in your slide deck.
5. You shall refrain from excessive use of animation, effects, and sounds.
6. You shall refrain from busy slide backgrounds.

Following those rules will save you a ton of time and effort along with receiving silent high fives and fist bumps from your audience.

With that out of the way, have your outline in front of you and read through each main point with their sub-point(s) and picture what image comes to mind after reading through it. Write that image down for each main point and for each sub-point if needed. That's the image you're going to use for your slides. If you have three main points, you should have five slides: introduction, main point 1, main point 2, main point 3, and the conclusion. You may have an outline slide. This is the easiest and most simplistic route.

If pictures are worth a thousand words, take advantage of that. Use the minimum amount of words as you can on each slide.

I know this approach may not work for everyone. You may have to add additional slides, graphs, charts, etc. However, the principle remains. If you need more than an image, do the bare minimum to get the job done. Make the simplest slides you can to get by and move on. It is more important to move on to actually speaking through your talk than to stress over what your slides look like. I'd rather you practice speaking and hope you have time to make your slides look better than work on your slides and hope you have time to practice speaking through them.

You might be thinking, *Why mostly images?*

Because slides are visual aids. They should simply be a visual representation of the message you want to get across to your audience. Each slide should have a purpose to enhance the points you want your audience to remember. If a slide doesn't serve a purpose, delete it.

Your slides should *enhance* the presentation; they should not *be* the presentation. Too many people put just about everything they want to say on their slides. If I can look through your slides and get the gist of your message without ever hearing you speak, what's your purpose as the speaker? What's the purpose of you to talk through your slides? To reiterate what the slides are saying?

If you put so much effort into your slides that the audience doesn't even need you than your speaking serves no purpose. Do not put all the responsibility of sharing the message on your slides. Do not try to take the attention off of you. This will actually make things worse for you.

When you depend on your slides to guide you through your talk, to present to the audience, to communicate on your behalf, you stop depending on yourself. You put your confidence in external factors instead of in your ability to speak. Do the opposite. Depend on yourself to give your talk. Build confidence in your ability to speak. Own the responsibility as the speaker. Believe in yourself, not your slides.

Don't worry if you don't feel confident or believe in yourself right now. The steps ahead will get you there.

Now that my slide rant is over, it's time for you to get to work. Depending on how much content you have, you might want to do an image/slide for each sub-point.

Once you're done, crank up the presentation software you're going to use and do online searches for images/graphics that came to mind for each point. Start copying and pasting those images into individual slides. Don't waste time searching for the "perfect" image. Find one that'll work and move on. If you have time after you are done working through your speech, then you can go back to fix your slides, make edits, or find better images. Set a timer for thirty minutes and get to work. Finish by adding a title slide, an outline slide if needed, titles to all the slides you add images to, and your conclusion/summary slide. Save it and get ready for the next leap. It's time to start speaking.

Go to chapter 8.

To-do Checklist:

- Use your outline to think of images/graphics that come to mind
- Search for those images/graphics online
- Use those images/graphics in your slides
- Make an introduction slide
- Make a conclusion/summary slide

7

ALREADY MADE SLIDES

I had a client who was new to her job tasked with giving a brief to the entire company on a new service to be rolled out to all current and future clients. You'd think they would want someone with experience with the new service to present it to the company. Instead, they chose the newest member who was absolutely terrified to speak in front of people.

She was handed a premade slide deck on the new service and a due date to present. There were over fifty slides on a topic she knew nothing about. As you can imagine, she was more than overwhelmed just thinking about where to even begin to prepare to give the presentation.

What you are about to discover is exactly what we did to quickly pinpoint the critical information on each slide to drastically cut down what she needed to know about the topic.

Later you will discover what we did to get her confidently prepared to present the material to her entire company.

To make sense of a presentation you have been given, quickly create an outline for your speech from your slides.

To do this, write out the key points for each slide in your slide deck. Leave some space at the top of the piece of paper for your introduction and go to the first slide where the real meat of the presentation begins. For the first slide, look through it and determine the main point it's trying to get through to the audience and write it down. Write any sub-points you think are necessary underneath the main point. Use as few words as possible. What you are writing down is the outline for your presentation, not a script to read from. Do the same for each slide.

If you are looking over a slide and the point it is trying to make is unclear, either quickly edit the slide to make it clear or decide to remove it. If it doesn't make sense to you, it certainly won't make any sense to your audience.

You will use this outline to start practicing your speech. The outline is the backbone of your entire presentation, not your slides. Never solely rely on the slides to guide your speech. Your slides are simply a visual aide—nothing more than a visual representation of the message you, the speaker, are trying to get across to your audience. If something goes glitchy with your slides before you speak or somewhere in the middle of your talk, what are you going to do if you were depending on your slides? Crash and burn most likely.

I'm going to show you how to practice to make the real thing so easy that you could crush it even if your slides go down in flames.

With an outline made for each slide, go to the top where you left a space and write in the structure of your introduction. You can use different methods, depending on why you're speaking. In some cases, a quick introduction of who you are followed by jumping right into the body of your speech is appropriate. In other cases, an introduction of who you are, why you're speaking, what you are going to speak about, and why the audience should care will be required. I'm counting on you to use your best judgement on how best to start your speech. Write at the top what you believe is needed or required for your introduction.

At the bottom of the page, you'll write the structure of your conclusion. Again, this will be different based on the reason you're speaking. Your conclusion could be a summary of your main points, closing thoughts, a call to action, requesting another round of applause for the bride and groom, or a thank you for the opportunity to speak. There are a lot of options to choose from.

Moving forward, consider your outline to be a living document, meaning it's going to change. At this point, you have not even used it to guide you through your talk. Your outline is simply a plan for your speech. Plans are great until you put them into action as you realize you want to make changes. That's perfectly normal. Keep that in mind.

Once you're done, you have everything you need to go ahead and start practicing speaking through your material. With your outline complete, head to chapter 8.

.   .   .

To-do Checklist:

- Pinpoint the purpose of each slide
- Write down the main point/sub-point(s) for each slide
- Leave room at the top of your introduction
- Add the introduction to your outline
- Add the conclusion to your outline

8

BEFORE YOU MOVE ON

Things to avoid and consume before you speak

1. Drink some water a few hours before you speak and drink some before you practice. There is something about being nervous while speaking that just sucks all the moisture out of your mouth and repurposes it as sweaty armpit stains. What a trash defense mechanism.

2. Try and stay away from coffee (or at least keep it to a minimum). It is a diuretic which makes you pee more often, absorb less water, and dehydrate faster. The exact opposite of what you want.

3. Stay away from sugar and dairy. Sugar can give you what I like to call "sticky spit," causing you to try and unsuccessfully swallow between every sentence while you speak. Dairy can make you mucous-ee. Gross. Both of these make it harder to speak for long periods of time. So if you drink coffee in the morning with milk and sugar . . . what a deliciously terrible trio.

Understanding my practicing method

I feel a need to stop you here before charging ahead. What's in the chapters ahead is so effective because of the unorthodox method laid out to prepare you to speak. I say unorthodox because it's the exact oppo-site of how most people prepare to speak for any occasion. Most people practice in comfortable envi-ronments where they can run through their talk in private. They do this with good intentions but a comfortable environment under minimum pressure does nothing for you and does nothing to prepare you for the real thing. Nothing.

People don't want to show anyone their talk in progress. Only when they've practiced enough to feel comfortable giving their talk in front of an audience of none, do they dare give it in front of anyone. Unfortunately, the first people to see the result of all that "practice" is typically the audience it was meant for.

This is one of the main reasons people are so afraid to speak in public. They practice in an environment void of pressure and wonder why they perform so poorly during the real thing.

Also, practicing the same way over and over in the same environment gets boring quickly.

If you want to perform under pressure, you have to practice under pressure. Remember that as you dive into what's to come. You will be instructed to do things when you don't feel ready, moving forward after just barely completing the current task. That is a good thing. This is designed specifically to keep you moving forward in discomfort, saving you time and continuously exposing you to performing outside your comfort zone. However, it is done in manageable steps so it doesn't feel like too much of a leap.

It is this combination of discomfort and not feeling ready that makes the results so extraordinary. It allows you to practice in conditions that feel far worse than the real thing. By the time you actually speak, not only will you be more than ready, but you'll be completely comfortable being uncomfortable. Let's do this!

Go to chapter 9.

9

SPEAK THROUGH YOUR OUTLINE

The time has come to finally speak through the outline of your speech. What you'll need:

1. Your outline or script
2. Your slides (if applicable)

Rules to follow moving forward:

1) You do not care about uhs, ums, awkward pauses, nervous ticks, losing your train of thought, stumbling over or mispronouncing words, or repeating yourself. You do not have time to worry about any of these things. You also don't have time to fix it either. These go away as you become more comfortable giving your talk. Anything you unintentionally do while speaking to a crowd that you would hardly ever do talking one-on-one with a close friend is none of your concern at this point.

2) When you start talking through your speech, do not stop! Don't do it! The first time you mess up, you'll be tempted to simply start over to get a better start. Do not do that. Keep going. Push through your mistake like nothing happened. I'd rather you flounder or stare silently at your outline for a minute to get your thoughts in order instead of starting over. You will not get the opportunity to start over during the real thing so practice like you are expected to perform. This trains you to push through the uncomfortable feeling of making mistakes without the option of turning back to start over.

When you are afraid of public speaking, you experience a fight or flight response. Use your practice to train yourself to not run back to the starting line when you mess up. Instead, fight through it and keep going. When you constantly stop and start over, you get really good at delivering the first few minutes of your speech while everything else is not practiced nearly as much. Pushing through allows for every section of your talk to get the same level of attention.

Working from an outline, if you are not used to it, can be tricky at first. If you followed my direction to not cram too many words, then your outline is just a skeleton of your speech. Of course, if you decided to write a script, then you have all the words. But this is one of the many reasons why outlines are better than scripts. At first, you may feel you need more words to work with. You'll feel that you need more to remind you of everything you need to say. But those gaps in your outline will come from you as all of that info is there, you just have to trust yourself that it will come to you when you need it.

For a lot of inexperienced speakers, they're used to depending on slides, or notecards, or scripts, or even memorizing everything they plan to say to get through their talk.

There is a fear that you'll have nothing to turn to if your mind goes blank in the middle of speaking. This is a common fear and one that comes from training yourself to depend on something other than yourself. Too often people use external cues as a safety net. Yes, it will feel uneasy letting go of your safety net, but I guarantee you this is the path worth taking. You develop a level of confidence that comes from truly knowing your material that you can't achieve while depending on something external to get you through.

What's laid out in this book is a way to get you to confidently know your material cold. You do that by using a bare-bones outline. Your outline is what you will use to practice, and as you practice, you will memorize your outline. This very structure of your speech will be solidified in your mind. This works best when you gradually commit it to memory as you speak through the material versus trying to memorize it first before trying to speak through it. Memorizing gradually as you speak through it allows each section of your outline to be associated with the content behind those sections to better recall information from memory.

So as you speak through your outline and you feel you don't need it, gradually stop looking at it to guide you through your talk. The less you need your outline, the more you will trust yourself to present the material, and the more confident you will become.

3) You will experience some resistance to getting started. This is normal and to be expected. Getting started is the hardest part, but this usually comes from having high expectations for the first few times you speak through your talk even though it's currently in a draft form. Lower your expectations on your performance.

I tell all of my clients who are having trouble getting started to speak ugly. Purposely be terrible. I'm positive you could pull that off. My clients, not surprisingly, do significantly better trying to be purposefully terrible.

4) Understand the first few rounds are going to be rough. You're working with a draft of what the final will look like. If at any point you're thinking your outline stinks, your slides stinks, your script stinks, or even the way you're presenting your material stinks, you are probably right. Overall, I'm sure it does stink but that will change. Each time you go through your entire talk, you'll make changes. You will remove some pieces of your speech that don't work, add pieces that are better, and make minor edits here and there.

The way you speak through your material will also change. You'll deliver it more comfortably but you'll also change how you run through your introduction, how you close it out, and you'll start adding transitions in between main points to help you flow from one part to the next. Just know that what you start with will not be what you present when it counts.

5) If you have slides, do your best to not look at them. Your slides are a visual aid for your audience. They are not for you. Let your outline guide you through your material.

Ready to begin

With that in mind, talk through your outline three times all the way through. Remember, it is a draft, getting started is the hardest, do not stop if you mess up, and purposefully be terrible. You are going to do great!

After you have gone through your talk three times, move on to chapter 10 to move to the next step. If your talk is longer than twenty to thirty minutes and you're short on time, consider skipping chapters 10 and 11 by going straight to chapter 12.

Pro Tip

As you go about your day, you will have little pockets of time where you are not doing much of anything whether you're eating, cooking, cleaning, commuting, showering, etc—tasks that you can pretty much do on autopilot. Since you don't have lots of time to prepare, you'll want to use those moments to run through your outline. I recommend you always have your outline on you in case you have an opportunity like those riddled through your day.

Given your particular circumstances, you may not get a chance to run through everything laid out in this book, but squeezing in practices while performing mundane tasks will add up to you getting a lot more practice running through your outline.

To-do Checklist:

- Speak through your outline three times
- Don't stop if you mess up
- Make edits as you see fit
- Keep your outline on you to run through it when you find time throughout the day

10

RECORD YOURSELF

S o you've run through your outline a few times and now it's time to step it up a notch.

Step 1: record yourself

Get out your phone, camera, or laptop and get ready to record yourself as you speak through your material.

If you don't have a way to record yourself, use a mirror, though I don't find this nearly as useful.

Record yourself standing up like you would give your talk. Remember, do not stop if you mess up. Keep going as if nothing happened. If you feel some resistance to getting started, that's a great sign. That feeling means you're uncomfortable and not 100 percent assured you can do this. Awesome! That's exactly what you're looking for. When you feel a lack of assurance and push through anyway, your growth and confidence accelerate; this is the perfect environment for such growth. Performing imperfectly during discomfort is a way more valuable experience than practicing perfectly in a comfortable environment ever will be.

Try to look into the camera, or the area behind the camera, as if the audience is there and use your outline as little as possible. If you are expecting to speak while standing up, practice delivering your talk standing up. A lot of people make the mistake of sitting down while practicing. Practice like you are expected to perform.

Same goes for your slides. Do your best to not look at them as you record yourself.

Step 2: review your recording

When you are finished, watch the recording but without any volume. While this may seem pointless, there's a good reason for it: I only want you to focus on what you are physically doing as you speak. It's time to see what you look like from the perspective of the audience. It can be uncomfortable. It can definitely be cringey but you need to do it. Uncomfortable is what we're looking for. You need to see what you're doing under stress. Are you making weird facial expressions? Does your demeanor say you are excited about what you're talking about or completely miserable? Do you have a weird tick or fidget, such as constantly putting your hand in your pocket, taking it out, putting it back in, and taking it back out? Do you sway back and forth while you talk?

I'm not expecting you to fix everything you find. I only want you to be aware of what you unintentionally do when you are nervous since you can't fix what you're not aware of.

After you finish reviewing the recording, go to chapter 11.

To-do Checklist:

- Find something to record yourself with
- Record yourself going through your talk
- Watch the recording without the volume on
- Make notes of anything you do that's distracting while you speak.

11

PUSH-UPS (IN A PUBLIC SPEAKING BOOK?)

C an you do a push-up? You know, like the exercise? You're probably thinking, *what does that have to do with public speaking?*

You will soon find out. If you can do a push-up, great! If you can't, hang tight, I've got something for you, too!

Give your speech while in the push-up position. Even if you have a long speech, do it anyway. Don't worry. I'll show you how to make it easier as it gets harder to hold the position.

Doing this does several things for you:

1) It uses up nervous energy. When we get nervous or scared to speak, we get this buildup of nervous energy that we often don't know what to do with. So while you're trying to give your talk, your body is looking for ways to channel that energy to use it. Next thing you know, you're talking like you're an auctioneer, you're swaying back and forth, and you're flailing your arms around with every word you make.

Some people manage to hold it in but not in a good way. The nervous energy builds up and instead of letting your body use it, you tense up trying to keep it all in. Next thing you know your knees start knocking, your hands begin to shake, and your voice starts to have an odd vibration effect when you speak. Whether you like it or not, your body will find a way to use that excess energy.

Tensing up your body also makes it really hard to breathe. Try it. Tense up your entire body, all of your muscles, and then try to take a deep breath. You can't do it, can you? When you're tense, you'll take shallow, choppy breathes as you try and speak.

Giving your speech in the push-up position forces you to use up that nervous energy so you can focus on how you deliver your talk. My clients are always surprised how calm, collected, and confident they sound while giving their talk in the push-up position.

2) You can't move. Remember all of those physical traits you noticed when you watched your recording? This exercise (pun intended) doesn't allow you to move around, to use your hands as you speak, to fidget, or anything like that. All you can do is hold the position and speak. It's incredible how much better you become when you are not subconsciously moving around so much. This allows you to experience what it's like to hold your ground, so to speak, while speaking.

3) It's physical stress. Performing under physical stress while giving your talk forces you to perform while under physical stress that far exceeds what you'll experience during the real thing. Like I mentioned before, a big piece of this sequence of steps is to train you harder than you are expected to perform.

If you haven't already, go ahead and get into position with your outline or script on the ground directly below your head and begin speaking.

You might be thinking *what about my slides? Do I flip through them while in the push-up position?*

That's easy to answer. You don't! You are not going to flip through them. They are not for you, remember? You will simply use your outline of your talk.

If you begin struggling to hold the position, switch to having your knees on the ground instead of your feet. This will make it easier. If that becomes challenging, find a bench or chair to put your hands on instead of having them on the ground with your outline on the bench or chair in front of you. If all else fails, prop yourself up against a wall and tape your outline to the wall in front of you.

For those who can't do a push-up, pick one of the easier versions and go from there. Also, I've never seen anyone hold the first position for their entire speech (unless it was really short). Everyone eventually drops to an easier version throughout their talk.

If an injury prevents you from holding a push-up position regardless of the difficulty level, consider doing a wall sit where you use your legs to brace your back up against a wall as if you're sitting on an invisible chair. This position is harder to hold for long periods of time. You may want to push yourself higher up the wall to make it easier. A reason this hold is not ideal is that it doesn't restrict your arms since you have to use at least one hand to hold up your outline. However, if you need to do it, then do it.

If you have an injury that prevents you from doing any of the exercises, skip this section and go straight to chapter 12.

To-do Checklist:

- Give your speech in the push-up position (or an easier position)
- Drop to an easier position until you get through your entire talk

AN AUDIENCE OF ONE

This is now no longer a solo mission. You now need to go find someone to present to. This can be your significant other, roommate, friend, neighbor, colleague, co-worker, etc. Anyone who can be your audience of one.

It may feel awkward asking someone to watch you present. Good! As you already know, that's exactly what we're looking for. Just be honest. Something like, "I've got a presentation coming up and I'm kind of nervous about it. Do you mind watching me present and giving me some feedback?"

I can just about guarantee they will say yes. Then again, you're probably not worried about them saying no. You're worried about what comes after they say yes: experiencing the uncomfortable feeling of going through your talk while someone stares at you as you pretend you're actually presenting to a room full of people.

This is where you kick the discomfort up a notch—whether you feel ready or not.

Use your outline as needed, don't look at your slides (if you have some), and have your audience of one time you. This a good time to see how long your presentation is, especially if you're aiming to stay within a certain time limit. I don't recommend timing your talk earlier since your talk will typically change drastically over the first handful of dry runs. By now, you have run through it several times, so you have a good idea of what's going to make it to the final version. Plus, you may end up speaking faster in front of an audience than you would alone.

When you are done speaking, ask for feedback and brace yourself for it. Some people can be very blunt with their feedback. Others will sugar coat their suggestions for improvement. Then there are some who will tell you that you're amazing no matter what and offer to put your handy work on the front of the fridge. Others won't hold back.

Some of the feedback will be useful and others will be better left unsaid. Either way, it is up to you to sift through it all and to not get butt hurt when someone points out a flaw, regardless if it's valid or not.

Any feedback you get about saying uhs, ums, fidgeting, or swaying back and forth, just make a note of it for awareness purposes only. You won't be able to intentionally fix most of those in the little time you have to prepare. Instead, you want to focus on feedback about your actual message: was there any piece that didn't make sense or a section that could use more clarity. Was there a point where you went way too far into the nitty-gritty details that went over your audience's head?

Most importantly, ask them what they thought was the purpose of your speech. If their answer aligns with the reason you're speaking (to inform, entertain, persuade, inspire, etc.), you're on the right track.

If this is for something like a eulogy or best man speech, you don't necessarily need feedback. What's important is getting the experience of speaking in front of somebody before the real thing.

To-do Checklist:

- Find someone to speak in front of
- Give your talk to them and time it
- Ask for feedback
- Make note of what you can improve on

13

DO SOMETHING UNPROFESSIONAL

One of the biggest struggles people have with public speaking is the difference between how they want to appear (like a professional) and how they actually perform. This gap causes so many people issues. They are so nervous to meet this high standard that they can't relax enough to achieve it. When the way you present yourself is nothing like you wanted, you feel worse than had you not had such a high standard to begin with. What's even more frustrating is that deep down you know you are fully capable of performing like a professional, but when all eyes are on you, things start to fall apart and you lose control.

Losing control is an uneasy feeling and doing it in front of a room full of people is more than enough to keep most people from ever wanting to speak in front of a crowd.

Do you want to know how to maintain control? Stop taking yourself too seriously! Stop trying to look professional!

When you stop taking yourself so seriously, you can finally relax. And when you're relaxed while speaking in front of an audience, you can be your genuine self—your true self. You might not have a lot of experience being "a professional" speaker. But I can guarantee that you have years of experience being you. This is where true confidence on stage comes from.

Do you want to know a foolproof way to instantly stop taking yourself so seriously? Do something completely unprofessional.

This is where things get silly, funny, and uncom-fortable. I want you to do something you could never bring yourself to do in front of people. This can come in many different flavors but one has consistently gotten results for my clients: speak through your speech with your tongue out. That's it. It's simple yet harder to do than you might think.

Go ahead and give your entire speech with your tongue out.

You'll probably think, *This is silly, why am I doing this? This feels stupid. There's no way this will help. There is no way I'm doing that.*

All of those reasons are the exact reason why you should. You are afraid to correlate an activity that you believe is supposed to resemble professionalism with acting silly, feeling stupid, or feeling embarrassed.

You need to let go of this image of how you're "supposed" to act, and this silly exercise is going to help you do it. Doing this will make the real thing feel like a piece of cake. Most importantly, it forces you to finally laugh at yourself as you try to go through your material. Soon, you can't help but smile.

I have all my clients take it a step further. Not only do they have to talk through their talk with their tongue out in front of me but they also have to do something way more embarrassing. My clients have to wear one of those little plastic mouthpieces that dentists use to hold their patient's mouths wide open while they speak. I wear one too and it's freakin' hilarious. They're laughing, I'm laughing, and we're both drooling all over the place. You want to know the result? My clients, who start out terrified to speak, completely destroy their next talk. Why? Because they finally got an opportunity to laugh and smile and let go of everything that was holding them back. They finally got to feel what it's like to speak and have fun. To confidently share a message. To not worry about whether or not they appeared to look professional but to boldly and vulnerably show who they truly are.

Remember that client I talked about who had to give a presentation to the entire company who was absolutely terrified? This is exactly what we did to prepare her and she absolutely crushed it.

When this finally clicks for my coaching clients, it's like watching a light turn on in their brains. They realize all their efforts trying to look like a professional were actually making things worse.

They also consistently pushed through even when they didn't feel ready, they put in the right work, and they trained harder than they were expected to perform. Just like you are experiencing now as you go through this book. So if you haven't already, speak with your tongue out. Laugh at yourself. Smile. Have fun. Feel yourself start to relax.

If you want to see some serious results, do it in front of someone. If you can do that, you will become unstoppable. What could phase you after that? Nothing.

Having fun yet? Good.

I use the tongue out method a lot. I've also stood on my desk in my underwear as I sang through my entire speech. It's ridiculous and fun once you get into it. Most importantly, it works.

When you're done, come back. Do not get distracted!

To-do Checklist:

- Give your speech with your tongue out

14

GO FIND SOMEONE ELSE

Is your tongue sore yet? If it is, don't worry. You're almost done. By now, you should know your outline frontward and backward. If not, you should be close. You should also be comfortable going through your slides without looking at them (if you have any). If you do look at them, it's only to make sure the correct slide is showing.

Your final task is to find someone else to present to, preferably a small group of people. This is your final dry run to push through the boundaries of your comfort zone before experiencing the real thing.

People often struggle with the task of asking multiple people to watch them speak. They get so caught up worrying about bothering people that they freeze and don't do anything at all. Stop thinking for once and just ask for their assistance. I've asked colleagues, bosses, co-workers, friends, family, and even random strangers for help to watch me speak and every time I'm surprised just how willing people are to help if I just buck up and ask for it.

You may be thinking *that's easy for you to say and do, you're a public speaking coach for crying out loud.*

That's a valid point but I still feel uncomfortable asking people for help to watch me speak.

Every time I get to the point that I need to ask a group of people to watch me speak, I feel a huge wave of resistance. I don't want to do it. Suddenly organizing my desk or responding to emails seems way more important. My brain is looking for a way out. Anything to distract me from what I need to be doing.

Quite frankly, it makes perfect sense. We don't naturally chase pain or discomfort. We do whatever we can to avoid it. Even the low level of pain from the discomfort of speaking feels like a threat that must be avoided. Even though I know with 100 percent certainty that I am not in danger, I still feel the pull to avoid it.

So to overcome that, I focus only on getting that first person. Then I ask that first person if they can help me find a few more. Now I've got a team of volunteers helping me find a group to speak to.

Go do it. Find someone. Find multiple people. It may not be easy, but it will be worth it. Put in the work now to make the real thing way easier.

Ask for feedback when you are done speaking, then come back and read through chapter 15 before you speak for real.

To-do Checklist:

- Find someone else to speak in front of (preferably a group)
- Ask for feedback

15

SHOW TIME

Ah, the day has finally come to give your talk. Twenty-four hours has almost past and you have made some serious headway in your very short amount of time. Hopefully, you followed the earlier advice to stay away from sugar, coffee, and dairy. Now, before you speak, I suggest you do the following:

1. Run through your talk one more time. At this point, this is just a review of your talk along with an opportunity to use up some built-up nervous energy that could get worse the closer it gets to go time.
2. Breathe. As you get nervous, your breathing will become shallow and more frequent. If

you can control your breathing, you can start to control your nerves. I have all of my clients take in a deep breath, gradually filling up the diaphragm and then the rest of their lungs. Hold for seven seconds. Release it naturally. Repeat. Do that for at least two minutes, and you'll be surprised how much better and more relaxed you feel.

3. Make sure you drink some water before you speak, just like you did before you practiced.

4. Give your speech. Crush it. Use your outline if you need to. Well done.

To-do Checklist

- Run through your speech
- Breathe when you start to feel nervous/anxious
- Crush your speech

CONCLUSION

You now have all the essential tools to crush your talk and any in the future. It has been an honor to walk you through the steps over the past twenty-four hours.

I leave you now that you have everything you need. I hope you have come to realize you are everything you need to be a great speaker: your genuine, authentic self.

Come find me if you need me.

Your coach,

Cody

Thanks again for choosing this book to guide you in crushing your speech in less than 24 hours.
I don't want you to forget about your free gifts.

The Public Speaking Panic Quick Start Checklist. This is the checklist I walk all my coaching clients through.

With it, you will discover how to implement the contents of this book even faster.

I also want to give you a copy of my bestselling book:
Stage Fight – How to Punch Your Fears of Public Speaking in the Face!

Either go to this URL: https://fearpunchingcody.com/publicspeakingpanicchecklist
or use the QR code for your free gifts:

You can also simply text **PANIC** to (678) 506-7543 to download your free Quick Start Checklist along with my bestselling book.

COULD YOU DO ME A SOLID?

Hey reader,

I hope you've gained something for investing your time going through *Public Speaking Panic.*

If you have benefitted in any way from reading this book, I'd love to hear from you.

Could you tell me what you thought about the book in a review?

A sentence or two would mean so freakin' much, you don't even understand.

Reviews are hard to get like those golden star stickers back in pre-school for good behavior. While Fred is sitting over there in the front row with 13 of those jokers, I've got my measly 1 for not wetting myself during nap time.

You can scan the QR code below that will take you straight to the review page.

Thank you!

Cody Smith is a speaker, Amazon Bestselling Author, and public speaking coach. He's particularly well equipped to transform the most unprepared and overwhelmed individual into a self-confident, battle tested stage crusher.

In his spare time, he loves nothing more than to play with his two daughters, spend time with his wife, and experiment to create the world's greatest cheesecake.

If you'd like to be coached by Cody or have him speak at your next event, reach out to him at the email below. He might even reply with a virtual fist bump.

Cody@fearpunchingcody.com

Printed in Great Britain
by Amazon

059